100% NATURAL

Hunt's®
TOMATOES

Favorite Tomato Recipes

Publications International, Ltd.

www.pilcookbooks.com

ISBN-13: 978-1-4127-7860-2
ISBN-10: 1-4127-7860-3

Manufactured in China

Pictured on the front cover: Classic Lasagna *(page 74).*

Preparation/Cooking Times: Preparation times are based on the approximate amount of time required to assemble the recipe before cooking, baking, chilling or serving. These times include preparation steps such as measuring, chopping and mixing. The fact that some preparations and cooking can be done simultaneously is taken into account. Preparation of optional ingredients and serving suggestions are not included.

Contents

Welcome to the Hunt's® Kitchens

Dear Cook,

Hunt's® tomatoes are 100 percent natural with no artificial ingredients or preservatives. When you reach for the familiar Hunt's red can, you are reaching for superior quality and the true tomato flavor that makes meals come alive.

FRESH-FROM-THE-VINE FLAVOR

Hunt's® whole and diced tomatoes go from the vine to can in a matter of hours. And only Hunt's uses a natural steam process to prepare and pack these tomatoes. The end results of the **FlashSteam™** process are the most natural canned tomatoes possible. Hunt's is the undisputed leader in tomatoes, and they continue to go the extra mile to bring you the best and most consistent quality possible. Try the fresh tomato taste of Hunt's in your favorite recipe today.

Hunt's has recipes for every occasion. Visit **www.hunts.com** to find your favorite.

Cooking Tips
From Hunt's®

All Hunt's whole and diced products are made with hand-selected 100% vine-ripened California tomatoes. Here are cooking tips for using specific Hunt's products.

Hunt's® Diced Tomatoes

Product Description: Peeled and uniformly diced, then packed in rich tomato juice for a full flavor.

Uses and Benefits: Excellent, convenient, ready-to-use product for a wide variety of recipes where a consistent tomato chunk is desirable. The chunky texture holds up well in cooking due to specially selected tomatoes. Available plain or with a variety of seasonings and flavors added for additional convenience and versatility. Great used as is or combined with paste or sauce for heartier sauces for meat, poultry or pasta.

Flavored varieties include Basil, Garlic & Oregano; Green Pepper, Celery & Onion; Mild Green Chilies; Roasted Garlic; Sweet Onions; Balsamic Vinegar, Basil & Olive Oil.

Sizes: Plain and Flavored 14.5 ounce and 28 ounce

Hints From Hunt's®

Add Interest and Texture—Try using diced tomatoes in place of, or in addition to, tomato sauce to add eye appeal, texture, your personal touch to favorite recipes and sauces.

Toss a Meal—Cook a pound of pasta and toss with 2 cans of Diced Tomatoes with Balsamic Vinegar, Basil and Olive Oil (add chunks of cooked chicken or sausage or drained small white beans, if desired). Top with freshly grated Parmesan cheese.

Super Soups & Stews—Add a can or two to soups and stews (homemade or prepared) and add color/eye appeal, chunky texture, rich flavor and broth… plus excellent nutrition.

Make Salsas Quickly, Conveniently, and Consistently—Make salsa anytime without the hassle of chopping tomatoes or worrying about the availability of fresh tomatoes.

Meals in Minutes—Top meat, chicken, seafood, pastas, and grains with piping hot flavored Hunt's® Diced Tomatoes for a quick, complete meal with minimum clean up.

"Speed Scratch"—Use a prepared spaghetti sauce but make it look more homemade and chunkier by adding diced tomatoes. Plus, it will extend the number of servings.

Hunt's® Diced Tomatoes in Sauce

Product Description: Peeled and uniformly diced, then packed in a rich tomato sauce for a full flavor and texture.

Uses and Benefits: Excellent, convenient, ready-to-use product for a wide variety of recipes where a consistent tomato chunk is desirable. Adds extra body for sauces, broths, and gravies. The chunky texture holds up well in cooking due to specially selected tomatoes.

Size: 14.5 ounce

Hints From Hunt's®

Add Texture and Body—Add to water-based soups to increase visual appeal by adding color to broth, appetizing texture with tomato chunks and increased body with the addition of tomato sauce.

Decrease Ingredients Used—If a recipe calls for a small can of diced tomatoes in juice plus a can of tomato sauce, try using 2 cans of Hunt's Diced Tomatoes in Sauce.

Great for Hearty Stews, Soups, Salsas—The added body of tomato sauce plus the tomato chunks make this an excellent ingredient for signature salsas, chowders, beef stew, chili, gumbos, and creole.

Hunt's® Crushed Tomatoes

Product Description: Specially selected, fresh, unpeeled tomatoes are crushed to create this product for many uses. The tomatoes are unpeeled to ensure a natural textured and fresh flavored product with bright red color.

Uses and Benefits: Great in sauces where a pulpy, full-bodied texture is desired; looks like fresh tomatoes that have been long-simmered and reduced.

Size: 28 ounce

Hints From Hunt's®

Add Body and Fresh Taste to Salsa—Use crushed tomatoes along with diced tomatoes in juice, chopped onions, and cilantro to make a salsa that tastes great and clings to chips for a burst of delicious taste in every bite.

Hunt's® Petite Diced Tomatoes

Product Description: Peeled and uniformly diced in smaller pieces, then packed in rich tomato juice for full flavor.

Uses and Benefits: Excellent, convenient, ready-to-use product for use where a smaller dice is desirable. The chunky texture holds up well in cooking due to specially selected tomatoes.

Size: 14.5 ounce

Hints From Hunt's®

More Tomato Pieces Ounce for Ounce—Because the dice is smaller, there are more pieces per ounce than regular diced tomatoes. Provides great flavor in every bite and good piece identity throughout finished dish.

Adds an Upscale Look—Try in salads to add a fresh taste and bold color accent that can be well distributed.

Hunt's® Stewed Tomatoes

Product Description: Peeled and thickly sliced, then blended with choice seasonings and vegetables.

Uses and Benefits: Excellent convenient product suitable to be used as is for a nutritious side dish or as a flavorful, versatile base for soups, stews, sauces and casseroles.

Also, available with no salt added.

Size: 14.5 ounce

Hints From Hunt's®

Great Easy Side Dish—Heat and serve as is, or, add sautéed sliced zucchini and onion for the easiest ratatouille ever.

Add Fresh Seasonal Touches for Year-Round Flair—Add fresh chopped, seasonal herbs like basil, oregano or parsley, then heat and eat. Or, combine with fresh garden vegetables like squash, green beans, spinach, sautéed mushrooms or grilled eggplant cut into chunks. Simmer and serve.

Hunt's® Tomato Paste

Product Description: Processed to remove seeds and skin, then concentrated to a "spoon-thick" consistency with the perfect balance of sweetness and acidity for a rich tomato flavor and deep red color.

Uses and Benefits: Perfect for adding thickness, body, color, and the richness of intense, fresh tomato flavor for a range of recipes. May be used alone, with other tomato products or diluted with broth, water, or wine.

Sizes: 6 ounce (also in Basil, Garlic and Oregano, and No Salt Added), 12 ounce, 18 ounce, and 29 ounce

Hints From Hunt's®

What To Do When You Only Need A Small Amount Of Paste—Open can at both ends; use lid on one end to push out paste onto plastic wrap. Wrap 'log' of paste tightly with plastic and freeze. When less than one can is needed, remove from freezer, unwrap and slice amount desired (½-inch from 6-ounce can equals about 2 tablespoons). Wrap tightly and return to freezer.

Quick Recipe Fix—Use paste like a bouillon cube; add a tablespoon or two to soups, sauces, slow cooker recipes, gravy or bottled salad dressing (especially no fat versions) to perk up flavor, color AND add body/richness.

Time-, Space-, and Money-Saving Substitutions—Substitute 1 can (6 ounce) Hunt's Tomato Paste PLUS 1 cup water in recipes that call for 1 can (15 ounce) tomato sauce *or* 2 lbs. fresh tomatoes, cooked, *or* 2 cups puree.

Make Marinara Sauce FAST—Blend 2 cans (6 ounce) tomato paste, 3 cups hot water and 2 cans (14.5 ounce) Hunt's Diced Tomatoes with Basil, Garlic, and Oregano together. Simmer 10 minutes. Use in place of prepared spaghetti, pasta, or marinara sauces.

Hunt's® Tomato Puree

Product Description: Processed to remove seeds and skin to yield a full-bodied puree with balanced, fresh tomato taste and color.

Uses and Benefits: Ideal for sauces when a full, fresh tomato taste is desired along with some extra body.

Sizes: 10.75 ounce and 29 ounce

Hints From Hunt's®

Add Body—Great in stews, chili, and soups to give more body to the sauce.

Rounds Out Flavor—Puree has a slightly sweet flavor that is ideal for blending flavors and a good addition to use with other tomato products like diced tomatoes or whole tomatoes to intensify flavors.

Hunt's® Tomato Sauce

Product Description: Lightly seasoned to yield a mild, but fresh tasting tomato sauce with bright red color.

Uses and Benefits: Use when a mild tomato flavor will enhance sauces that do not need extra body added. Helps blend other flavors and adds nutrition, color, and flavor. Good in most soups, great with a variety of meats as well as rice, pasta, noodles, and other grains.

Sizes: 8 ounce (also available in Basil, Garlic and Oregano, No Salt Added, and Roasted Garlic).

Hints From Hunt's®

Give Vegetable Soup Your Signature—Add to vegetable soup for a nice background color and fresh, healthy taste. Helps increase the nutrition in every bowl.

It's Too Hot!—Add to chili or other highly seasoned soups, stews, and dishes to smooth out and give a well blended taste.

Pizza in a Hurry Without the Delivery—Top English muffins or pre-baked pizza shells with tomato sauce, then sprinkle with Italian seasoning and top with pepperoni slices, if desired. Finish with shredded mozzarella cheese. Bake in a toaster oven until cheese is bubbling.

Hunt's® Whole Peeled Tomatoes

Product Description: Firm, flavorful tomatoes are hand-selected for taste, texture, and bright red color, then peeled for use.

Uses and Benefits: Ideal for cooks who like to create tomato-based dishes exactly to their specification. Piece size and shape can be controlled by cook for the ultimate in creativity—coarsely crushed, random chunks, whatever is desirable to make signature dishes and sauces.

Sizes: 14.5 ounce (also available in No Salt Added) and 28 ounce

Hints From Hunt's®

Cutting Tips—If tomatoes need to be cut into chunks, use kitchen shears and cut while still in can, eliminating a bowl to wash.

Coarsely Crushed Tomatoes—Wear plastic gloves and squeeze tomatoes through fingers into bowl or pan to ensure a non-uniform crush.

Adds Authentic Look and Feel—Keep Italian-inspired Bolognese, Arrabbiata, and Puttanesca sauces unique and authentic using whole peeled tomatoes. Also great for Margherita Pizza and other classic dishes.

Starters & Sauces

Tomato-Cheese Bruschetta

Fresh slices of bread brushed with olive oil then toasted until crisp and golden brown topped with tomato, onion, basil, and melted cheese

Hands On: 20 minutes
Total: 20 minutes
Makes: 12 servings (2 slices each)

Ingredients Needed:

- 1 loaf (16 ounces) crusty Italian bread, cut diagonally into 24 slices
- ½ cup olive oil
- 1 can (14.5 ounces) **Hunt's® Petite Diced Tomatoes**, drained
- ½ cup chopped sweet onion
- 2 tablespoons chopped fresh basil leaves
- ½ teaspoon finely chopped garlic
- ¼ teaspoon salt
- ⅛ teaspoon ground black pepper
- 2 cups shredded part-skim mozzarella cheese

Steps to Prepare:

PREHEAT oven to 400°F. Brush both sides of each bread slice with oil. Place slices on baking sheet; bake 5 minutes on each side, or until golden brown.

COMBINE tomatoes, onion, basil, garlic, salt and pepper; mix well. Spoon evenly divided portions onto each slice of toast. Sprinkle with cheese.

BAKE 3 minutes, or until cheese is melted.

Mexican Salsa

A chunky, zesty South-of-the-Border delight

Hands On: 10 minutes
Total: 10 minutes
Makes: 2 cups

Ingredients Needed:

- 1 can (14.5 ounces) **Hunt's® Petite Diced Tomatoes, undrained**
- ¼ cup chopped onion
- 1 small jalapeño pepper, seeded and chopped
- 2 tablespoons chopped fresh cilantro
- 1 clove garlic, minced
- ½ teaspoon granulated sugar
- ¼ teaspoon salt
- ¼ teaspoon ground black pepper

Steps to Prepare:

COMBINE all ingredients in small bowl.

COVER and refrigerate 2 hours prior to serving.

Hints from Hunts.

Great for a simple snack with chips, served over potatoes or rice, or as a zesty condiment for Mexican dishes.

Chili Lime Shrimp

A succulent and spicy appetizer or small plate fare

Hands On: 10 minutes
Total: 10 minutes
Makes: 4 servings (about 5 pieces of shrimp each)

Ingredients Needed:

- 2 tablespoons Asian chile garlic paste
- 2 tablespoons **Hunt's® Tomato Paste**
- 1 pound medium raw shrimp, peeled and deveined
  Fresh limes, cut into wedges

Steps to Prepare:

WHISK together chile garlic paste and tomato paste in a small bowl.

COOK shrimp in oiled hot wok or large skillet 5 minutes or until just pink.

STIR in tomato mixture; toss to coat. Squeeze lime juice over shrimp.

Hints from **Hunt's.** Experiment by combining Hunt's® Tomato Paste with other flavored pastes and sauces and spreading over beef, chicken, or fish.

Tomato Pesto Tart

A flavorful and festive appetizer...ready in minutes!

Hands On: 10 minutes
Total: 30 minutes
Makes: 9 servings

Ingredients Needed:

1   **sheet puff pastry, thawed according to package directions**
     PAM® Original No-Stick Cooking Spray
½   **cup prepared pesto**
1   **cup (4 ounces) shredded mozzarella cheese, divided**
1   **can (14.5 ounces) Hunt's® Whole Tomatoes, sliced**

Steps to Prepare:

UNFOLD puff pastry on a floured surface. Cut off ½- to ¾-inch strips from each side. Place pastry square on a baking sheet sprayed with cooking spray. Wet edges of pastry square lightly with water. Lay strips of pastry on top of pastry square, forming a pastry shell with raised edges. Press strips lightly to seal to pastry shell.

SPREAD pesto evenly across bottom of pastry shell; sprinkle with ½ cup cheese, tomato slices, and remaining ½ cup cheese.

BAKE in preheated 400°F oven for 17 to 20 minutes or until golden brown. Serve immediately.

Hints from Hunt's

No need to fear working with puff pastry. It is easy to thaw and use. Do not confuse puff pastry with phyllo pastry, which is more delicate.

Special Pomodoro Sauce

*This chunky tomato sauce is bursting
with fresh flavor and texture*

Hands On: 20 minutes
Total: 20 minutes
Makes: 4 servings

Ingredients Needed:

- ¼ **cup virgin olive oil**
- 1 **medium onion, chopped**
- 1 **large red bell pepper, chopped**
- 2 **teaspoons minced garlic (4 cloves)**
- 1 **can (14.5 ounces) Hunt's® Petite Diced Tomatoes, drained**
- 1 **tablespoon red wine vinegar**
- 1 **package (⅔ ounces) fresh basil, thinly sliced (about ½ cup)**
- ½ **cup slivered almonds, toasted**

Steps to Prepare:

HEAT oil in a large skillet over high heat; add onion, bell pepper, and garlic. Cook about 8 to 9 minutes, stirring frequently, or until onion is soft and liquid is evaporated to develop flavor.

BLEND in tomatoes, vinegar, and basil; cook about 1 minute or until heated through. Stir in almonds. Season to taste.

SERVE over pasta, seafood, or chicken as a main dish. Or, serve on slices of French bread or wrapped in lettuce leaves for an appetizer.

Hints from Hunt's

To toast, place almonds on a small baking sheet; bake in a preheated 350°F oven for 10 minutes or until golden brown. To have toasted almonds on hand for quick use, prepare more almonds than needed. Cool; then place in a resealable freezer bag and store in freezer for later use.

Chunky Tomato Alfredo Linguine

Nothing is more satisfying than this creamy Alfredo sauce updated with a tomato twist

Hands On: 15 minutes
Total: 20 minutes
Makes: 6 servings (about 1⅓ cups each)

Ingredients:

1   can (14.5 ounces) **Hunt's® Diced Tomatoes in Juice, undrained**
1   can (6 ounces) **Hunt's® Tomato Paste**
1   container (10 ounces) refrigerated Alfredo Sauce
1   pound uncooked linguine pasta, cooked and kept warm

Steps to Prepare:

COMBINE tomatoes and paste in a microwave-safe bowl; heat on HIGH 2 to 3 minutes, stirring halfway through.

FOLD in Alfredo sauce; toss with linguine.

Hints from **Hunts.** Keep plenty of convenient Hunt's® Diced Tomatoes in Juice on hand to use in place of fresh tomatoes, and save the time of chopping and cleaning up afterwards with no sacrifice in fresh flavor.

Salads & Sides

Rustic Tuscany Bread

*The savory flavors of tomatoes and cheese make
this warm baked bread extraordinary*

Hands On: 20 minutes
Total: 2 hours 45 minutes
Makes: 6 servings

Ingredients Needed:

1	**pound frozen bread dough**
1	**tablespoon olive oil**
¼	**teaspoon salt**
¼	**teaspoon cracked black pepper**
1	**can (14.5 ounces) Hunt's® Diced Tomatoes with Basil, Garlic & Oregano, drained**
½	**cup (2 ounces) shredded Cheddar cheese**
½	**cup (2 ounces) shredded mozzarella cheese**
	PAM® Original No-Stick Cooking Spray

Steps to Prepare:

THAW bread dough; let rise according to package directions.

ROLL dough out to a 12×10-inch rectangle. Brush dough lightly with olive oil; sprinkle with salt and pepper. Layer well-drained tomatoes and cheeses over dough. Fold dough in thirds over filling. With a sharp knife, make three diagonal cuts, about 2 inches apart, on top of dough through first layer. Repeat with second set of cuts in opposite direction, crisscrossing first cuts.

PLACE dough on a baking sheet coated with cooking spray. Bake in a preheated 400°F oven for 25 minutes or until golden brown.

Fiesta Taco Salad

You won't be able to get enough of this
lively Mexican-inspired salad

Hands On: 20 minutes
Total: 20 minutes
Makes: 6 servings

Ingredients Needed:

1   **pound lean ground beef or ground turkey**
1   **can (14.5 ounces) Hunt's® Diced Tomatoes in Juice, undrained**
1   **package (10 ounces) frozen whole kernel corn, thawed**
1   **package (1 ounce) taco seasoning mix**
6   **to 9 cups salad greens (about 10 ounces)**
4   **ounces tortilla chips**
    Sliced ripe olives, sliced green onions, shredded Cheddar cheese, and/or sour cream (optional)

Steps to Prepare:

COOK meat in a large skillet over medium-high heat until crumbled and no longer pink; drain. Add tomatoes, corn, and seasoning mix; blend well. Bring to a boil; reduce heat and cook, uncovered, 8 minutes, stirring occasionally.

PLACE about 1½ cups of greens on each serving dish. Top with meat mixture. Arrange tortilla chips around lettuce.

GARNISH with olives, onions, cheese, and/or sour cream, if desired.

Chicken, Spinach & Mango Salad with Warm Tomato Vinaigrette

This luscious, colorful salad is full of interesting flavors and textures

Hands On: 25 minutes
Total: 25 minutes
Makes: 4 servings

Ingredients Needed:

- 2 teaspoons olive oil
- 12 ounces boneless, skinless chicken breast, cut into bite-size pieces
- 1 can (14.5 ounces) **Hunt's® Petite Diced Tomatoes in Juice, undrained**
- ¼ cup prepared **French salad dressing**
- 1 tablespoon **seasoned rice vinegar**
- 1 bag (5 ounces) fresh baby spinach leaves (about 4 cups)
- 2 ripe, medium mangos, pitted, cut into bite-size pieces
- 2 ripe, medium avocados, pitted, cut into bite-size pieces
- 4 slices bacon, cooked, crumbled (about ¼ cup)

Steps to Prepare:

HEAT oil in a large skillet over medium-high heat. Add chicken; cook until lightly browned, stirring occasionally, about 4 minutes.

ADD tomatoes; bring to a boil. Reduce heat to low. Cook, uncovered, about 5 minutes or until chicken is no longer pink. Add dressing and vinegar; heat through.

ARRANGE equal amounts of spinach, mangos, and avocados on each serving plate. Top each with chicken-tomato mixture. Sprinkle each with bacon. Serve immediately.

Cool and Crisp Albacore Pasta Salad

Delicious summery salad of tender pasta,
vegetables and flaky albacore

Hands On: 15 minutes
Total: 1 hour 15 minutes
Makes: 6 servings (1⅓ cups each)

Ingredients Needed:

8	ounces dry bow tie (farfalle) pasta, uncooked
1	can (28 ounces) **Hunt's® Petite Diced Tomatoes**, drained
1	can (12 ounces) albacore tuna, drained and flaked
1	large cucumber, peeled, seeded and chopped
¾	cup shredded carrots
¾	cup mayonnaise
½	cup sliced green onions
½	cup thinly sliced fresh basil leaves
1	teaspoon lemon pepper seasoning
¼	teaspoon salt
8	large lettuce leaves, optional

Steps to Prepare:

COOK pasta according to package directions. Drain; rinse with cold water.

COMBINE tomatoes, tuna, cucumber, carrots, mayonnaise, onions, basil, lemon pepper and salt in large serving bowl. Add cooled pasta. Gently toss until well blended.

COVER; refrigerate 1 hour. Serve on lettuce leaf-lined salad plates, if desired.

Hints from

Great Substitute: Hunt's Diced Tomatoes, drained, or Hunt's Whole Peeled Tomatoes, cut up and drained, can be substituted for the Hunt's Petite Diced Tomatoes.

Tomato Risotto

Traditional creamy risotto without all the fuss

Hands On: 30 minutes
Total: 30 minutes
Makes: 6 servings

Ingredients Needed:

- 3 **tablespoons butter**
- 1 **cup sliced green onions**
- 1½ **cups uncooked Arborio rice or medium-grain white rice**
- 1 **can (14.5 ounces) Butterball® Chicken Broth**
- 1 **can (14.5 ounces) Hunt's® Diced Tomatoes with Green Pepper, Celery and Onions, undrained**
- ¾ **cup grated Parmesan cheese**
- ¼ **teaspoon salt**
- ¼ **teaspoon ground black pepper**

Steps to Prepare:

MELT butter in a large skillet over medium heat, about 2 minutes; add green onions and sauté for about 1 minute. Stir in rice; cook an additional 2 minutes.

ADD broth and tomatoes. Bring to a boil, cover and reduce heat to low; simmer for 20 minutes.

SIMMER, uncovered, 5 minutes, stirring occasionally. Remove from heat; blend in cheese. Season with salt and pepper.

Chilled Tomato & Vegetable Pasta Salad

Colorful pasta mixed with chunky tomatoes, crisp vegetables, feta cheese and a zesty Italian dressing

Hands On: 20 minutes
Total: 1 hour 20 minutes
Makes: 9 servings (about 1 cup each)

Ingredients Needed:

1	pkg (12 ounces) dry tri-color rotini pasta, uncooked
1	can (14.5 ounces) **Hunt's® Diced Tomatoes**, drained
1	medium cucumber, quartered lengthwise, thinly sliced
1	pkg (4 ounces) crumbled feta cheese
1	can (3.8 ounces) sliced ripe olives, drained
½	cup shredded carrots
½	cup chopped roasted red peppers
¼	cup finely chopped red onion
1	cup zesty Italian dressing
¼	cup pine nuts, toasted (optional)

Steps to Prepare:

COOK pasta according to package directions; drain. Rinse with cold water. Place in large bowl.

ADD tomatoes, cucumber, cheese, olives, carrots, red peppers and onion; mix lightly. Add dressing; toss to coat. Cover.

REFRIGERATE at least 1 hour prior, or until chilled. Sprinkle with pine nuts, if desired.

Soups, Stews & Chili

Garden Vegetable Soup

Satisfying soup in a matter of minutes

Hands On: 5 minutes
Total: 20 minutes
Makes: 4 servings

Ingredients Needed:

- 1 bag (16 ounces) frozen vegetables with pasta and garlic seasoned sauce
- 1 can (14.5 ounces) **Hunt's® Diced Tomatoes in Juice, undrained**
- 2 cans (14 ounces each) chicken broth

Steps to Prepare:

COMBINE all ingredients in a medium saucepan.

BRING to a boil. Reduce heat; simmer until heated through.

Roasted Tomato Tortilla Soup

*A classic Mexican soup jazzed up
by the addition of fire roasted tomatoes*

Hands On: 15 minutes
Total: 40 minutes
Makes: 6 servings

Ingredients Needed:

- 1 tablespoon **Pure Wesson® Canola Oil**
- 1 cup frozen whole kernel corn
- 1 cup chopped red onion
- ½ cup chopped celery
- 2 teaspoons minced jalapeño pepper
- 1 tablespoon minced garlic
- 3½ cups reduced-sodium chicken broth
- 1 can (14.5 ounces) **Hunt's® Fire Roasted Diced Tomatoes,** drained
- 1½ cups shredded cooked chicken breast
- ½ cup diced queso fresco cheese
- ¾ cup sour cream
- 2 ounces white tortilla chips, coarsely broken
- 3 tablespoons chopped fresh cilantro

Steps to Prepare:

HEAT medium saucepan over medium-high heat; add oil, corn, onion, celery and jalapeño. Cook and stir 3 to 5 minutes or until vegetables are tender. Add garlic; cook 1 minute or until aromatic.

ADD broth, drained tomatoes and chicken. Cook, uncovered, over medium heat 10 to 12 minutes or until hot and flavors have blended.

DIVIDE cheese equally between each soup bowl. Add 1 cup soup to each. Top with equal amounts of sour cream, tortilla chips and cilantro.

Queso fresco cheese may be found in most Latino markets or in the supermarket's ethnic/gourmet cheese section. Monterey Jack cheese may be substituted. For a restaurant-style presentation, make fried tortilla strips by cutting 5 (8-inch) flour or corn tortillas in quarters and then into ⅛-inch-wide strips. Heat 3 cups canola oil in heavy-bottomed skillet 10 to 15 minutes or until oil reaches 350°F. Cook strips 2 to 3 minutes or until lightly browned and crisp; drain on paper towels. Season with salt, if desired. Store leftover strips in an airtight container up to one week.

Tomato Basil Crab Bisque

This elegant, luscious soup will delight your friends and family

Hands On: 15 minutes
Total: 20 minutes
Makes: 4 servings

Ingredients Needed:

- 1 tablespoon margarine or butter
- ½ cup chopped onion
- ½ cup **Butterball® Chicken Broth**
- 1 can (8 ounces) **Hunt's® Tomato Sauce with Roasted Garlic**
- 1 cup half-and-half
- 1 cup coarsely chopped cooked crabmeat
- ¼ teaspoon salt
- ⅛ teaspoon ground black pepper
- ¼ cup chopped fresh basil leaves

Steps to Prepare:

MELT margarine in a Dutch oven or a medium saucepan over medium-high heat. Add onion and cook until golden, about 2 minutes.

ADD the broth, tomato sauce, half-and-half, crabmeat, salt and pepper. Bring just to a boil, reduce heat, cover tightly and simmer 5 minutes. Sprinkle with basil before serving.

Heartwarming
Beef Stew Skillet

*All the heartiness of a slow-cooked beef stew
in less than 30 minutes!*

Hands On: 20 minutes
Total: 30 minutes
Makes: 4 servings

Ingredients Needed:

- 1 tablespoon **Pure Wesson® Vegetable Oil**
- 1 pound boneless beef sirloin, seasoned with salt and black pepper, cut into 1-inch cubes
- 1 can (14.5 ounces) **Hunt's® Stewed Tomatoes**, undrained
- 2 packages (.87 ounces each) brown gravy mix
- 2 cups cold water
- 1 tablespoon Worcestershire sauce
- 1 bag (16 ounces) frozen stew vegetables, thawed

Steps to Prepare:

HEAT oil over medium-high heat in a large skillet. Add beef, in batches, if necessary, to brown. Remove beef; set aside.

ADD tomatoes, gravy mix blended with cold water, Worcestershire sauce and vegetables; bring to a boil.

RETURN beef to skillet; reduce heat. Cook, covered, 10 minutes, or until vegetables are tender, stirring occasionally.

Cool and Easy Gazpacho

*Gazpacho is a refreshing summer soup that is
served cold; great as a snack or as a meal*

Hands On: 15 minutes
Total: 1 hour 15 minutes
Makes: 6 servings

Ingredients Needed:

- 2 cans (14.5 ounces each) **Hunt's® Diced Tomatoes in Juice, undrained**
- 3 medium red bell peppers, washed, seeded, cut into chunks (about 2 cups)
- 2 cucumbers, peeled, seeded, cut into chunks (about 2 cups)
- ⅓ cup chopped red onion
- ¼ cup red wine vinegar
- ¼ cup seasoned rice vinegar
- 3 tablespoons virgin olive oil
- 2 tablespoons fresh chopped parsley
  Shredded Cheddar cheese, seasoned croutons (optional)

Steps to Prepare:

PLACE all ingredients into the bowl of a food processor fit with metal blade or in a blender. Work in batches, if needed.

PULSE ingredients until coarsely chopped and blended. Do NOT purée.

COVER and refrigerate at least 1 hour before serving. Season to taste. Garnish with shredded Cheddar cheese, seasoned croutons, and/or more chopped parsley, if desired.

Very Veggie Chili

Spicy vegetarian chili with two varieties of beans and colorful vegetables — bell pepper, corn, and carrots

Hands On: 15 minutes
Total: 4 hours 15 minutes
Makes: 6 servings

Ingredients Needed:

- 1 can (14.5 ounces) **Hunt's® Fire Roasted Diced Tomatoes with Garlic,** undrained
- 1 can (8 ounces) **Hunt's® Tomato Sauce-No Salt Added**
- 1 can (15 ounces) Ranch Style Beans, undrained
- 1 can (15 ounces) **Van Camp's® Red Kidney Beans,** drained, rinsed
- 1 small yellow onion, chopped
- 1 medium green bell pepper, chopped
- 1 cup frozen whole kernel corn
- 2 medium carrots, sliced
- 1 tablespoon **Gebhardt® Chili Powder**
- ½ teaspoon ground red pepper
- 12 corn tortillas (6 inch), warmed

Steps to Prepare:

PLACE all ingredients, except tortillas, in 4-quart slow cooker; stir to combine.

COVER; cook on HIGH 1½ to 2 hours or on LOW 3 to 4 hours.

SERVE chili with tortillas.

Italian Favorites

Penne Pasta Casserole

The entire family will love this meaty, cheesy pasta dish

Hands On: 20 minutes
Total: 45 minutes
Makes: 6 servings

Ingredients Needed:

- 12 ounces uncooked penne pasta (about 3½ cups)
- 1 pound lean ground beef or ground turkey
- 1 large onion, chopped (about 1 cup)
- 1 can (14.5 ounces) **Hunt's® Diced Tomatoes with Basil, Garlic & Oregano**
- 1 can (6 ounces) **Hunt's® Tomato Paste**
- ½ cup water
- 3 cups (12 ounces) shredded mozzarella cheese
  PAM® Original No-Stick Cooking Spray

Steps to Prepare:

COOK pasta according to package directions; set aside. Meanwhile, cook ground beef and onion in a large skillet until beef is crumbled and no longer pink; drain. Stir in tomatoes, tomato paste, and water. Season to taste; heat through.

COMBINE cooked pasta with meat-tomato mixture and 2 cups mozzarella cheese in a 13×9×2-inch baking dish coated with cooking spray. Top evenly with remaining 1 cup cheese.

BAKE, uncovered, in a preheated 350°F oven for 20 to 25 minutes or until heated through and cheese is melted.

Chunky Tomato Sauce with Bucatini Pasta

An easy-to-make chunky tomato sauce loaded with fresh veggies served over fun-shaped pasta

Hands On: 35 minutes
Total: 35 minutes
Makes: 4 servings

Ingredients Needed:

12	ounces dry bucatini or spaghetti pasta, uncooked
	PAM® Original No-Stick Cooking Spray
½	cup julienned zucchini
½	cup julienned yellow bell pepper
¼	teaspoon kosher salt
2	tablespoons extra virgin olive oil
2	cups chopped red bell pepper
1	cup chopped yellow onion
2	tablespoons minced garlic
2	cans (14.5 ounces each) **Hunt's® Petite Diced Tomatoes, undrained**
¾	cup thinly sliced fresh basil
2	tablespoons red wine vinegar
	Freshly shredded Parmesan cheese, optional

Steps to Prepare:

COOK pasta according to package directions. Meanwhile, spray large nonstick skillet with cooking spray. Place over medium-high heat 1 minute. Add zucchini, yellow bell pepper and salt. Cook and stir 2 minutes or until vegetables are crisp-tender. Remove from skillet; keep warm.

ADD oil to skillet. Add red bell pepper, onion and garlic; cook 8 to 10 minutes, or until onions are tender, stirring frequently.

ADD undrained tomatoes, basil and vinegar. Cook and stir 3 minutes or until hot.

SERVE tomato sauce over pasta. Top with reserved vegetables; sprinkle with Parmesan cheese, if desired.

Hints from Hunt's

To julienne vegetables, cut them into thin, match-like pieces, about 1½ inches long. This can be done with a chef's knife or using a piece of equipment called a mandoline.

Margherita Pizza

A classic thin-crust pizza generously topped with tomatoes, thinly sliced fresh mozzarella, and basil all drizzled with fruity olive oil

Hands On: 30 minutes
Total: 5 hours
Makes: 2 pizzas; 8 servings (2 slices each)

Ingredients Needed:

PAM® Olive Oil No-Stick Cooking Spray
1 **pound frozen bread dough**
1 **can (28 ounces) Hunt's® Whole Peeled Tomatoes,** drained
2 **tablespoons yellow cornmeal**
2 **tablespoons all-purpose flour**
8 **ounces fresh mozzarella cheese, thinly sliced, patted dry with paper towels**
3 **tablespoons extra virgin olive oil**
Fresh cracked black pepper
1 **package (⅔ ounce) fresh basil, leaves torn**

Steps to Prepare:

SPRAY medium bowl with cooking spray; add frozen dough. Spray dough with cooking spray. Loosely cover bowl with plastic wrap. Place on counter for 4 to 5 hours or until dough doubles in size. (Time will vary depending on temperature of kitchen.) Punch down dough.

PREHEAT oven to 400°F. Place tomatoes in large strainer or colander placed in sink. Break tomatoes into bite-size chunks by hand. Continue draining tomatoes while working with dough.

SPRAY two 12-inch pizza pans with cooking spray. Lightly sprinkle each with cornmeal; set aside. Cut dough in half. Dust work surface lightly with flour. Roll each dough piece into a 10-inch circle. Place each on a prepared pizza pan.

PLACE tomato pieces evenly over both pieces of dough leaving about ½ inch of edge clear. Top each pizza equally with sliced mozzarella. Drizzle lightly with olive oil then season with fresh pepper.

PLACE each pan on separate racks in oven. Bake 15 minutes; remove from oven. Quickly sprinkle each evenly with torn basil leaves. Rotate position of pizzas in oven. Bake another 5 to 10 minutes or until crust is golden brown on top AND bottom. Cut each pizza into 8 slices.

Hints from Hunt's

Fresh pizza dough may be available in your market. Follow recommendations for handling dough accordingly. Many pizza pans tend to deflect the heat while baking resulting in a pale, underbaked crust. If possible, use dark pans. Or, if available, use perforated pizza pans to ensure a golden brown top and bottom crust. In a hurry? Use two ready-to-use thin-crust pizza shells in place of frozen dough. Top as described above. Bake according to pizza shell package directions.

Savory Steak Stroganoff

*Dress up ordinary beef stroganoff by using steak
in place of ground beef*

Hands On: 30 minutes
Total: 30 minutes
Makes: 4 servings

Ingredients Needed:

- 8 ounces uncooked **NO YOLKS** or regular egg noodles
- 1 tablespoon olive oil
- 1 pound top sirloin steak, cut into ¼×2-inch strips, seasoned with salt and pepper
- ¼ cup white vinegar
- 1 medium onion, thinly sliced (about ½ cup)
- 12 ounces fresh mushrooms, sliced
- 1 can (15 ounces) **Hunt's® Tomato Sauce**
- ½ cup sour cream

Steps to Prepare:

COOK noodles according to package directions; drain and keep warm.

HEAT oil in a large nonstick skillet over medium-high heat. Add half of the steak and cook until no longer pink, stirring constantly. Set aside; keep warm. Repeat with remaining steak and set aside; keep warm.

ADD vinegar, onion, and mushrooms to skillet and cook until liquid is reduced, about 5 minutes. Add tomato sauce and reserved steak with any accumulated juices. Bring to a boil. Reduce heat to low; simmer, uncovered, 5 minutes.

REMOVE from heat. Stir ½ cup of hot tomato sauce from skillet into sour cream; blend well. Stir back into skillet. Serve over hot cooked noodles.

Spinach Lasagna Roll-ups with Tomato Coulis

Al dente lasagna noodles generously filled with spinach and feta cheese served with a delicious basil-infused tomato sauce

Hands On: 1 hour
Total: 1 hour 30 minutes
Makes: 6 servings

Ingredients Needed:

PAM® Original No-Stick Cooking Spray
9   dry lasagna noodles, uncooked

Tomato Coulis:
1   tablespoon olive oil
1   cup chopped red onion
1   tablespoon minced garlic
3   cans (14.5 ounces each) **Hunt's® Diced Tomatoes,** undrained
¼   cup thinly sliced fresh basil
½   teaspoon salt
½   teaspoon ground black pepper

Filling:
1   tablespoon olive oil
2   tablespoons minced shallots
3   packages (10 ounces each) frozen chopped spinach, thawed, squeezed dry
½   teaspoon salt
½   teaspoon ground black pepper
¼   teaspoon ground nutmeg
9   tablespoons crumbled feta cheese

Steps to Prepare:

PREHEAT oven to 350°F. Spray 13×9-inch baking dish with cooking spray. Cook lasagna noodles for about 6 minutes in salted, boiling water (or until pliable but still firm). When done, rinse with cold water, drain. Spray noodles with cooking spray to prevent sticking until ready to fill.

MEANWHILE, make Tomato Coulis. Heat oil in medium saucepan over medium heat 1 minute. Add onions and garlic; cook 4 minutes, stirring occasionally, or until onion is tender. Add undrained tomatoes; cook over medium-low heat 30 minutes (sauce should be gently bubbling around edge of pan). Remove from heat; add basil, salt and pepper. Working in batches, place coulis in blender container and purée until smooth. Place coulis in baking dish; set aside.

MAKE Filling: Heat oil in large skillet over medium-high heat 1 minute. Add shallots; cook 3 minutes, stirring occasionally, or until tender. Blend in well-drained spinach, salt, pepper and nutmeg. Cook and stir 3 minutes or until heated through. Remove from heat.

PLACE plastic wrap on work surface. Lay out lasagna noodles. Top each with equal amounts of spinach mixture (about ⅓ cup). Spread spinach evenly over each noodle leaving last 2 inches uncovered. Sprinkle 1 tablespoon feta over spinach on each noodle. Roll up each starting with the covered end. Carefully cut each roll-up in half and place ruffled-edge facing up in dish. Cover dish with aluminum foil. Bake 30 to 35 minutes or until sauce is bubbling and roll-ups are hot.

TO SERVE, spread ½ cup hot coulis in each shallow bowl; top with 3 roll-ups. Remaining sauce may be served on side.

Hints from Hunt's

Coulis [koo-LEE] is a term for a thick sauce or purée.

Pasta Arrabbiata

Pasta Arrabbiata is a wonderful rich and spicy pasta dish
that can be made and enjoyed in just under an hour

Hands On: 10 minutes
Total: 40 minutes
Makes: 8 servings

Ingredients Needed:

½ **cup virgin olive oil**
4 **teaspoons fresh minced garlic (about 5 cloves)**
1 **can (28 ounces) Hunt's® Petite Diced Tomatoes in Juice, undrained**
1 **can (29 ounces) Hunt's® Tomato Puree**
2 **teaspoons crushed red pepper**
½ **teaspoon dried oregano leaves**
¼ **teaspoon salt**
1 **pound uncooked penne pasta**
½ **cup freshly shredded Parmigiano Reggiano***
¼ **cup thinly sliced fresh basil**

*If not available, substitute a good quality freshly shredded Parmesan cheese.

Steps to Prepare:

HEAT oil in a 6-quart saucepan over medium heat. Add garlic; sauté about 3 minutes or until garlic is golden brown. Blend in diced tomatoes and puree; bring to a boil. Reduce heat to low; stir in crushed red pepper, oregano, and salt.

COOK, uncovered, for about 20 minutes, stirring occasionally. Meanwhile, prepare pasta according to package directions. Drain, reserve ½ cup cooking water.

PLACE pasta and reserved water in the saucepan; sprinkle with cheese. Add basil to sauce; pour 2 cups of sauce over pasta. Toss well to combine. Serve pasta with additional sauce.

One-Dish Meals

BBQ Skillet

Tender pork strips in a tangy BBQ sauce

Hands On: 5 minutes
Total: 30 minutes
Makes: 4 servings

Ingredients Needed:

- 1 pound boneless pork loin chops, cut into thin strips
- 2 tablespoons **Pure Wesson® Vegetable Oil**
- 1 medium onion, cut into thin strips
- 2 cans (8 ounces each) **Hunt's® Tomato Sauce**
- ½ cup **Hunt's® BBQ Sauce**
- 2 tablespoons packed brown sugar
  Hot cooked noodles or rice (optional)

Steps to Prepare:

COOK pork in a large skillet over medium-high heat until no longer pink; remove from pan; keep warm. Heat oil in skillet. Add onion strips; cook until soft.

BLEND in tomato sauce, BBQ sauce, and brown sugar. Add pork; mix well. Cover; reduce heat to low and cook for 15 minutes.

REMOVE lid; cook an additional 5 minutes or until sauce thickens. Serve over noodles or rice, if desired.

Slow-Cooked Pot Roast

Tender pot roast with red potatoes and
carrots in a savory tomato sauce

Hands On: 20 minutes
Total: 8 hours 20 minutes
Makes: 4 servings

Ingredients Needed:

- 1 tablespoon **Pure Wesson® Vegetable Oil**
- 1 tablespoon all-purpose flour
- ½ teaspoon ground black pepper
- 1 pound boneless beef chuck roast, well trimmed, cut into large pieces
- 2 medium red-skinned potatoes, cut into 2-inch pieces
- 1 cup sliced carrots
- ½ cup chopped onion
- 2 teaspoons minced garlic
- ½ cup lower sodium beef broth
- 2 tablespoons Worcestershire sauce
- 1 can (14.5 ounces) **Hunt's® Stewed Tomatoes,** undrained
- 5 tablespoons **Hunt's® Tomato Paste No Salt Added**
- ½ teaspoon granulated sugar

Steps to Prepare:

HEAT oil in large nonstick skillet over medium-high heat. Combine flour and pepper in shallow dish; coat meat with mixture. Place meat in skillet and brown all sides; transfer to 4-quart slow cooker. Add potatoes, carrots, onion and garlic.

STIR together broth, Worcestershire sauce, undrained tomatoes, tomato paste and sugar in medium bowl. Pour over meat and vegetables.

COOK on LOW 8 hours or HIGH 4 hours.

Beef Curry Skillet

Curry lovers and novices alike will love the perfectly blended taste of sweet and spicy in this dish

Hands On: 15 minutes
Total: 40 minutes
Makes: 6 servings

Ingredients Needed:

- 3 teaspoons curry powder, divided
- ½ teaspoon salt
- ¼ teaspoon ground red pepper
- 1 pound sirloin steak, thinly sliced*
- 2 tablespoons **Pure Wesson® Vegetable Oil**
- 1 large onion, chopped (about 1 cup)
- 1 can (14.5 ounces) **Hunt's® Diced Tomatoes in Juice**, undrained
- 1 can (14.5 ounces) beef broth
- 1 cup uncooked long-grain rice
- ½ cup raisins
- ½ teaspoon garlic powder
- 3 tablespoons slivered almonds, toasted

Steps to Prepare:

BLEND 2 teaspoons curry powder, salt, and red pepper together. Sprinkle evenly over steak. Heat oil in a large skillet over medium-high heat. Add steak; cook for about 5 minutes, stirring frequently, or until no longer pink.* Remove from pan; keep warm.

ADD onion to pan; cook about 5 minutes or until soft. Blend in remaining 1 teaspoon curry powder, tomatoes, broth, rice, raisins, and garlic powder. Bring to a boil; reduce heat to low. Cover; cook for 20 minutes or until rice is tender.

STIR steak back into rice mixture. Cover; let stand for 5 minutes. Top with almonds.

*Cook steak in 2 batches, if needed, to help the meat brown, not boil, in excess liquid.

Tomato Fideo Dinner

This is truly a one-dish meal;
the pasta does not require precooking!

Hands On: 20 minutes
Total: 30 minutes
Makes: 4 servings

Ingredients Needed:

    Salt and black pepper
1   **pound sirloin steak, thinly sliced**
¼   **cup Pure Wesson® Vegetable Oil, divided**
8   **ounces uncooked fideo* pasta, broken into 1-inch pieces**
1   **tablespoon minced garlic**
3   **cans (8 ounces each) Hunt's® Tomato Sauce**
3   **cups frozen broccoli florets, thawed and drained**

*Fideo is a very thin pasta similar to angel hair, primarily available in the West and Southwest; it can be purchased coiled or "broken." Substitute angel hair or vermicelli if not available.

Steps to Prepare:

SEASON steak with salt and pepper. Heat 1 tablespoon oil in a wok or large skillet over medium-high heat; cook steak about 3 to 4 minutes or until browned and no longer pink, stirring frequently. Remove from pan; keep warm.

ADD remaining oil, pasta, and garlic to wok. Carefully toss pasta in oil to coat; cook over medium heat until pasta is golden brown, stirring constantly. Stir in tomato sauce until pasta is well coated. Cover; reduce heat to low. Cook about 10 minutes or until pasta is tender.

COMBINE steak and broccoli with pasta; toss together. Cover; cook on low until heated through.

Hints from

For a quick and delicious Mexican side dish, eliminate the steak and broccoli, then cook the pasta in the oil, garlic, and tomato sauce as described.

Saucy Porcupine Meatballs

Kids and adults alike will love these; serve with extra rice

Hands On: 10 minutes
Total: 30 minutes
Makes: 6 servings

Ingredients Needed:

2   cans (8 ounces each) **Hunt's® Tomato Sauce**
2   tablespoons packed brown sugar
1   pound extra-lean ground beef
¼   cup quick-cooking rice
1   teaspoon Worcestershire sauce
1   egg, beaten
    Salt and black pepper

Steps to Prepare:

POUR tomato sauce into a large skillet. Add sugar; mix until dissolved.

COMBINE beef, rice, Worcestershire sauce, and egg in a large bowl; season with salt and pepper. Mix until well blended. Form into 1-inch balls; place into the skillet.

SPOON some of the sauce over the meatballs. Cook over medium heat until sauce begins to bubble. Cover; reduce heat to low. Cook for 20 minutes or until meat is no longer pink.

Pasta Pizza Bake

All the flavors of pizza with a pasta crust

Hands On: 15 minutes
Total: 40 minutes
Makes: 8 servings

Ingredients Needed:

- 8   ounces uncooked angel hair pasta
- 1   pound Italian sausage links, casings removed
- 1   can (14.5 ounces) **Hunt's® Diced Tomatoes with Basil, Garlic & Oregano**, undrained
- 1   can (6 ounces) **Hunt's® Tomato Paste**
- 2   cups (8 ounces) shredded mozzarella cheese, divided
- 2   large eggs, beaten
- 2   tablespoons Parmesan cheese (optional)
      PAM® Original No-Stick Cooking Spray

Steps to Prepare:

COOK pasta according to package directions; rinse under cold water to cool. Drain well; set aside. Cook sausage in a large nonstick skillet over medium-high heat for 5 minutes or until meat is crumbled, browned, and no longer pink; drain. Blend in diced tomatoes and tomato paste; heat through. Remove from heat; fold in 1 cup of mozzarella cheese.

WHISK together eggs and Parmesan cheese in a large bowl. Add pasta; toss until it is well coated. Spray a 13×9×2-inch baking dish with cooking spray. Press coated pasta evenly into bottom of baking dish.

POUR sausage mixture evenly over pasta. Sprinkle with remaining 1 cup mozzarella cheese. Bake in preheated 350°F for 32 to 35 minutes or until hot, crust is set, and cheese is melted. Let stand for 5 minutes before serving.

Creamy, Cheesy Chicken and Noodles

Creamy, cheesy & easy!

Hands On: 10 minutes
Total: 25 minutes
Makes: 6 servings

Ingredients Needed:

- 1 **pound boneless, skinless chicken breasts, cut into 1-inch chunks**
- 1 **medium onion, chopped**
- 1 **can (6 ounces) Hunt's® Tomato Paste**
- 3 **cups water**
- 3 **cups (about 5 ounces) uncooked extra-wide egg noodles**
- 1 **container (10 ounces) refrigerated Alfredo sauce**
- 1 **package (6 to 9 ounces) prewashed fresh spinach leaves**

Steps to Prepare:

COOK chicken and onion over medium-high heat in a nonstick 6-quart saucepan until chicken is no longer pink and onion is soft. Blend in paste and water.

ADD noodles; stir to blend. Bring to a boil; reduce heat to low. Cook, uncovered, 10 to 12 minutes or until noodles are tender.

BLEND in Alfredo sauce and spinach. Cover and cook over medium-low heat, stirring once, until spinach wilts and sauce is heated through. Season to taste.

Classic Lasagna

Hearty layers of flavorful meat, cheese and seasoned tomato sauce between al dente lasagna noodles baked to bubbling perfection

Hands On: 45 minutes
Total: 2 hours
Makes: 12 servings

Ingredients Needed:

9   uncooked lasagna noodles (about 8 ounces)
    PAM® Olive Oil No-Stick Cooking Spray
1   pound Italian pork sausage
1   pound ground round
1   medium onion, chopped
3   cloves garlic, minced
1   can (28 ounces) **Hunt's® Crushed Tomatoes**
1   can (14.5 ounces) **Hunt's® Diced Tomatoes with Basil, Garlic & Oregano**, undrained
4   tablespoons chopped fresh flat-leaf parsley, divided
½   teaspoon fennel seeds
½   teaspoon ground black pepper, divided
¼   teaspoon salt
2   cups part-skim ricotta cheese
1   cup shredded Romano cheese, divided
2   eggs, beaten
2   tablespoons thinly sliced fresh basil
3   cups shredded part-skim mozzarella cheese, divided

Steps to Prepare:

PREHEAT oven to 350°F. Cook lasagna noodles according to package directions. Drain and rinse with cool water to stop cooking. Meanwhile, spray large saucepan with cooking spray. Heat over medium-high heat until hot; add sausage and ground round. Cook and stir 5 minutes to crumble meat.

ADD onion and garlic to pan. Continue cooking 8 to 10 minutes or until meat is no longer pink and onion is tender. Drain meat mixture well. Add crushed and undrained tomatoes, 1 tablespoon parsley,

fennel seeds, ¼ teaspoon pepper and salt. Bring meat mixture to a boil. Reduce heat; cook uncovered over medium-low heat 10 minutes, stirring occasionally.

PLACE ricotta, ¾ cup Romano cheese, eggs, remaining parsley, basil and remaining pepper in medium bowl; blend well. Set aside.

ASSEMBLE LASAGNA: Spray 13×9-inch glass baking dish with cooking spray. Spread 1 cup meat sauce evenly over bottom of dish. Place 3 lasagna noodles over sauce, top with 2 cups meat sauce, half of ricotta cheese mixture and 1 cup mozzarella cheese. Repeat layers ending with a layer of noodles topped with sauce and the remaining mozzarella and Romano cheeses.

SPRAY underside of aluminum foil with cooking spray; cover dish tightly with foil. Bake 45 minutes. Remove foil and bake another 15 minutes or until cheese melts and sauce is bubbling. Let stand 10 minutes before serving.

Main Dishes

Seafood Veracruz

Fresh taste, fast, and delicious!

Hands On: 10 minutes
Total: 30 minutes
Makes: 4 servings

Ingredients Needed:

- 1 **can (8 ounces) Hunt's® Tomato Sauce**
- ½ **cup chunky tomato pico de gallo or salsa**
- 1 **pound fresh fish fillets (4 pieces)**

Steps to Prepare:

COMBINE sauce and pico de gallo in a small bowl.

DIVIDE fish fillets on 4 individual sheets of foil; top with tomato mixture. Seal foil to form packets.

PLACE packets on a baking sheet and bake in a preheated 450°F oven for 20 minutes.

Cod with Soba Noodles in Spicy Tomato Broth

Tender, moist cod served over soba noodles and napa cabbage in a spicy tomato broth seasoned with ginger and red pepper

Hands On: 25 minutes
Total: 50 minutes
Makes: 6 servings

Ingredients Needed:

4	ounces soba (Japanese buckwheat noodles), uncooked
2	tablespoons **Pure Wesson® Vegetable Oil**
1	tablespoon grated fresh ginger
2	teaspoons minced garlic
6	small cod fillets (about 4 ounces each), patted dry
1	teaspoon kosher salt
¼	teaspoon ground black pepper
1	can (14.5 ounces) **Hunt's® Petite Diced Tomatoes,** undrained
1	can (14 ounces) reduced-sodium chicken broth
2	teaspoons soy sauce
½	teaspoon crushed red pepper flakes
2	tablespoons lime juice
2	tablespoons chopped fresh basil
1	tablespoon chopped fresh cilantro
1	teaspoon granulated sugar
½	teaspoon toasted sesame oil
4	cups thinly sliced napa cabbage
¼	cup chopped green onion

Steps to Prepare:

COOK soba noodles according to package directions; cool and set aside.

HEAT vegetable oil in large skillet over medium-high heat. Sauté ginger and garlic about 30 seconds or until fragrant.

SEASON cod with salt and black pepper. Add cod to skillet and cook about 2 minutes per side or until lightly browned.

STIR in undrained tomatoes, broth, soy sauce and red pepper flakes. Bring mixture to a boil. Reduce heat to low, cover and simmer 20 minutes or until cod flakes easily with fork. Gently remove cod from skillet; set aside.

ADD lime juice, basil, cilantro, sugar and sesame oil to skillet; stir to combine. Add cabbage and reserved soba noodles. Simmer, uncovered, 1 to 2 minutes, or until cabbage is tender.

DIVIDE noodle mixture among 6 serving bowls; top each with piece of cod. Ladle additional broth over cod and noodles. Garnish with green onions. Serve immediately.

Hints from Hunt's

Soba noodles can be found in the ethnic or specialty section of your local grocery store. If unavailable, whole wheat vermicelli or angel hair pasta are great substitutes.

Rack of Lamb
with Vegetable Tagine

Fragrant, flavorful vegetables seasoned with cumin, ginger, cinnamon, paprika, mint, and cilantro served with moist, tender rack of lamb

Hands On: 30 minutes
Total: 1 hour, 8 minutes
Makes: 4 servings

Ingredients Needed:

½	cup reduced-sodium chicken broth
1	tablespoon lemon juice
1	tablespoon honey
2	teaspoons paprika
1	teaspoon ground cumin
1	teaspoon minced garlic
½	teaspoon ground ginger
¾	teaspoon kosher salt, divided
¼	teaspoon caraway seeds
¼	teaspoon ground cinnamon
½	teaspoon ground black pepper, divided
1	can (14.5 ounces) **Hunt's® Petite Diced Tomatoes,** undrained
½	cup diced butternut squash
½	cup diced zucchini
½	cup finely chopped onion
¼	cup diced red bell pepper
¼	cup finely chopped turnip
1¼	pounds frenched rack of lamb, 8 chops
2	tablespoons olive oil
2	teaspoons chopped fresh Italian (flat-leaf) parsley
2	teaspoons chopped fresh mint leaves
2	teaspoons chopped fresh cilantro

Steps to Prepare:

PREHEAT oven to 400°F. Combine broth, lemon juice, honey, paprika, cumin, garlic, ginger, ¼ teaspoon of the salt, caraway seeds, cinnamon and ¼ teaspoon of the black pepper in small bowl.

PLACE undrained tomatoes, squash, zucchini, onion, bell pepper and turnip in 13×9-inch baking dish. Pour broth mixture over vegetables; toss to coat.

COVER dish with aluminum foil. Bake 25 to 30 minutes or until vegetables are crisp-tender. Remove foil; bake 10 minutes more or until fork tender.

MEANWHILE, sprinkle lamb with the remaining salt and pepper. Heat oil in large skillet over medium-high heat until hot. Add lamb; cook 5 to 8 minutes or until golden brown. Remove from skillet; keep warm.

STIR parsley, mint and cilantro into vegetable mixture. Place lamb on vegetables; bake 15 minutes more for medium-rare (145°F) or 20 minutes more for medium (160°F). Let lamb stand 5 minutes before cutting into chops. Serve lamb with vegetables.

Hints from Hunt's

Use a regular stainless steel or aluminum skillet for the best browning when preparing the lamb. Nonstick skillets typically do not brown as well. Serve the lamb and vegetables with couscous to carry out the Moroccan influence. Recipe may be doubled or tripled if needed.

Mini Meatloaves

Serve this family favorite with savory potatoes

Hands On: 5 minutes
Total: 30 minutes
Makes: 6 servings

Ingredients Needed:

- 1 **pound lean ground beef**
- 1 **large egg, beaten**
- 1/2 **cup plain bread crumbs**
- 2 **cans (8 ounces each) Hunt's® Tomato Sauce, divided**
  Salt and black pepper
  PAM® Original No-Stick Cooking Spray
- 3 **tablespoons brown sugar**

Steps to Prepare:

MIX together beef, egg, bread crumbs, and 1 can tomato sauce in medium bowl; season with salt and pepper. Line a lipped baking sheet with foil. Coat with cooking spray. Form meat mixture into 6 mini loaves on pan.

BLEND sugar and remaining 1 can tomato sauce in small bowl. Pour tomato mixture evenly over tops of loaves.

BAKE meatloaves in a preheated 375°F oven for 25 minutes, or until no longer pink in center. Cool for 5 minutes before serving.

Tex-Mex Fish Tacos

Warm corn tortillas filled with pan-grilled white fish, a crisp and colorful jicama-vegetable blend, plus an 'anytime-of-the-year' tomato salsa

Hands On: 45 minutes
Total: 45 minutes
Makes: 4 servings

Ingredients Needed:

Fish

1	pound pollock or cod fillets, thawed if frozen
¼	teaspoon kosher salt
¼	teaspoon ground black pepper
	PAM® Grilling Spray

Salsa

1	can (14.5 ounces) **Hunt's® Petite Diced Tomatoes**, drained
⅓	cup finely chopped red onion
1	tablespoon minced jalapeño pepper
1	tablespoon chopped fresh cilantro
2	teaspoons minced garlic
2	tablespoons fresh lime juice
1	tablespoon extra virgin olive oil
1	teaspoon granulated sugar
¼	teaspoon kosher salt
¼	teaspoon ground black pepper

Tacos

1	cup julienned jicama
1	cup shredded napa cabbage
¼	cup shredded carrot
12	white corn tortillas (6 inch), heated
1	large avocado, cut into 24 slices

Steps to Prepare:

PREPARE FISH: Sprinkle fish with salt and black pepper. Spray grill pan with grilling spray; heat over medium-high heat until hot. Place fish in pan and cook 5 to 7 minutes on each side or until fish flakes easily with fork. Cool slightly and shred.

PREPARE SALSA: Combine all salsa ingredients in medium bowl; set aside.

COMPLETE TACOS: Combine jicama, cabbage and carrot in medium bowl. Place 2 tablespoons fish in middle of each tortilla. Top with about ¼ cup jicama mixture, 2 tablespoons salsa and 2 slices avocado. Fold in half; serve immediately.

Fire-Roasted Tomato Quesadillas

Crisp quesadillas filled with fire-roasted tomatoes, corn, black beans and Chihuahua cheese accented with fresh lime juice and cilantro

Hands On: 30 minutes
Total: 30 minutes
Makes: 6 servings

Ingredients Needed:

- 1 can (14.5 ounces) **Hunt's® Fire Roasted Diced Tomatoes,** drained
- ⅔ cup frozen whole kernel corn, thawed
- ⅔ cup Ranch Style Black Beans, drained and rinsed
- ⅓ cup chopped white onion
- 2 tablespoons finely chopped fresh cilantro
- ½ teaspoon garlic powder
- ¼ teaspoon kosher salt
- ¼ teaspoon ground cumin
- ¼ teaspoon ground red pepper
- 1 teaspoon lime juice
- 2 cups (8 ounces) shredded Chihuahua or Monterey Jack cheese
- 6 (8-inch) flour tortillas
  Lime wedges and sour cream, optional

Steps to Prepare:

MAKE 'salsa': place drained tomatoes in large bowl; mash into smaller pieces with fork. Mix in corn, beans, onion, cilantro, garlic powder, salt, cumin, red pepper and lime juice.

ASSEMBLE quesadillas by sprinkling ⅓ cup cheese over half of each tortilla; top each with ¼ cup 'salsa' (reserve remaining). Fold each tortilla in half over filling; set aside.

HEAT large nonstick skillet over medium heat. Cook quesadillas 2 to 3 minutes on each side or until cheese melts and tortilla is lightly browned.

CUT each quesadilla into 3 wedges. Serve each with remaining 'salsa.' Add a lime wedge and sour cream, if desired.

Monterey Jack cheese may be substituted for Chihuahua cheese, a Mexican melting cheese.

Easy Cheesy Enchiladas

You'll crave these cheesy chicken enchiladas
after you've tried them once

Hands On: 20 minutes
Total: 50 minutes
Makes: 6 servings

Ingredients Needed:

3   cans (8 ounces each) **Hunt's® Tomato Sauce**
1   cup plus 1 tablespoon water, divided
2   tablespoons chili powder
3   cups (12 ounces) shredded, cooked chicken
1   medium onion, chopped
12 white corn tortillas
3   cups (12 ounces) shredded Cheddar cheese, divided
    PAM® Original No-Stick Cooking Spray

Steps to Prepare:

COMBINE tomato sauce, 1 cup water, and chili powder in a medium saucepan. Cook over medium-high heat until sauce comes to a boil. Reduce heat to low; simmer, uncovered, 10 minutes, stirring occasionally. Meanwhile, place chicken, onion, and 1 tablespoon water in a large nonstick skillet. Cook over medium-high heat until the onion softens.

WRAP tortillas in moist paper towels. Place on a microwave-safe plate; heat on HIGH power for 45 to 60 SECONDS or until warm and softened. Remove from oven; keep wrapped.

FILL each tortilla with 2 tablespoons cheese and ¼ cup chicken mixture. Roll up; place seam side down in a 13×9×2-inch baking dish coated with cooking spray. Repeat with remaining tortillas. Cover evenly with sauce; sprinkle with remaining cheese. Seal pan with foil. Bake in a preheated 400°F oven for 30 minutes or until cheese melts and sauce is bubbling.

Shrimp Creole

Succulent shrimp in a savory sauce made with peppers, onions, celery, tomatoes, and Creole seasoning

Hands On: 40 minutes
Total: 40 minutes
Makes: 8 servings (1 cup each)

Ingredients Needed:

- 2 tablespoons **Pure Wesson® Vegetable Oil**
- 1 large onion, chopped
- 1 large red bell pepper, chopped
- 1 large green bell pepper, chopped
- 1 cup chopped celery
- 1 small jalapeño pepper, seeded and finely chopped
- 2 cloves garlic, minced
- 2 tablespoons Creole seasoning
- 1 pound extra-large shrimp, peeled and deveined
- 1 can (14.5 ounces) **Hunt's® Whole Peeled Tomatoes,** undrained, coarsely chopped
- 1 can (6 ounces) **Hunt's® Tomato Paste**
- Hot cooked rice (optional)

Steps to Prepare:

HEAT oil in large saucepan over medium-high heat. Add onion, bell peppers, celery, jalapeño pepper, garlic and seasoning; mix well. Cook 5 minutes, or until vegetables are crisp-tender, stirring frequently.

STIR in shrimp; cook 5 minutes, or until shrimp turn pink, stirring frequently. Add tomatoes with their liquid and the tomato paste; mix well. Bring to a boil over high heat. Reduce heat to low; simmer 10 minutes, stirring occasionally. Serve over hot cooked rice, if desired.

Substitution Chart

If your recipe calls for:	You can use instead:
1 pound fresh tomatoes, cooked	1 (8-ounce) can Hunt's® Tomato Sauce
2 pounds fresh tomatoes, cooked	1 (6-ounce) can Hunt's® Tomato Paste plus 1 cup water
1 cup tomato purée	1 (8-ounce) can Hunt's® Tomato Sauce
2 cups tomato purée	1 (6-ounce) can Hunt's® Tomato Paste plus 1 cup water
Tomato juice	Equal parts Hunt's® Tomato Sauce and water
1 (15-ounce) can tomato sauce	1 (6-ounce) can Hunt's® Tomato Paste plus 1 cup water
1 pound can whole or stewed tomatoes	1 (6-ounce) can Hunt's® Tomato Paste plus 1 cup water
1 (10-ounce) can tomato soup	1 (8-ounce) can Hunt's® Tomato Sauce plus ¼ cup water

Index